Tiktok Crash Book: A Hands-On, From Zero To Hero In Tiktok

SADANAND PUJARI

Published by SADANAND PUJARI, 2024.

Table of Contents

Copyright 1

About.. 2

Introduction... 3

From 0 to $10,000: YouTube vs TikTok......................... 10

2 Secrets To Get Tik Tok Followers And Views Fast! 17

5 Ultra-Powerful Tips to Make Even MORE Money on TikTok! 23

4 Ways to Find Lucrative Affiliate Programs That Pay Up to $1,000 Per..29

My Story - How My Account Got BANNED Because of Bullies on TikTok 36

How to RECOVER Your TikTok Account Step-By-Step 39

2 TIPS for TikTok 42

Copyright

Copyright © 2024 by **SADANAND PUJARI**

All rights reserved. No part of this book may be reproduced, scanned, or distributed in any printed or electronic form without permission. Please do not participate in or encourage piracy of copyrighted materials in violation of the author's rights. Purchase only authorized editions.

Tiktok Crash Book: A Hands-On, From Zero To Hero In Tiktok

First Edition: Jun 2024

Book Design by **SADANAND PUJARI**

About

Whether you're looking to boost your personal profile or hoping to generate revenue for your business, you'll want to be on TikTok.

The world's fastest growing social media platform, TikTok has around 800 million monthly active users. It's more popular than Instagram. Plus, it's the only place where new users can go viral overnight. In other words, it's a marketing opportunity you don't want to shy away from.

In this Book, we'll take you from complete newbie to a bonafide TikTok pro. You'll learn how to create a personal or business account that users will want to engage with, and how to conjure up an entertaining TikTok post. Growing your account is also on the agenda. In fact, we'll show you how to get 10,000 followers within 30 days without using dodgy bots or buying followers. We'll also reveal exactly how TikTok's algorithm works, so you can ensure your efforts are seen by your target audience. And we'll teach you the many ways you can make money from your TikTok account.

You don't need any kind of a following to get started with this Book — just a smartphone and a desire to participate in one of the most fun forms of social media. Got both? Then get ready to grow your profile.

Introduction

Hello, my friend, what if I told you that making money through TikTok is very simple, if you just give me five minutes of your time, I will show you six step strategy, how you can make tens of thousands of dollars by using TikTok in just five minutes, you will learn the strategy how Jonathan Montoya, Asgard, Jane Thornhill and other people have made tens of thousands of dollars just by creating sold 15 seconds videos on TikTok. And when you have finished this, will you have a strategy that you can start, by the way, to make money on? TikTok. But with this video, I want to remind you that don't over complicate the process. Making money through TikTok is very simple.

Just follow these six steps that you are going to find out soon before we dive into the first one. Remember to sum up the life for this video. If you find this valuable and feel free to share this with your friends who also want to make money online, step number one is to download the Tic-Tac application and create your own profile. This takes approximately 30 seconds and this whole process takes approximately five to maximum ten minutes. So this is very fast and simple, creating a profile takes maybe 10 seconds and then you just add some relevant picture of the profile and you are good to go. Step number two is to decide the topic that you want to talk about.

TikTok. And actually, you don't even need to talk. If you don't want, you can just add text and you don't really even need to show your face. There are many different ways you can make money by using TikTok, but when you are choosing a topic for your profile, I recommend that you choose something that you are interested in, something that you are passionate about, something that you want to share with the world. For example, there was one person who was passionate about history, so he created videos about the First World War, Second World War and other historic things. Then there was another man who was interested in relationships like men and women and all these things. So he created tips for young men and all this kind of stuff.

Then I'm interested in making money online and helping people with these things. So I created a profile where I teach people different ideas about making money online. So to something that you are passionate about, if you are playing football to football, if you love basketball to basketball, just pick one topic that you are going to talk about on your profile. That was the second step. Then the third step is to take a look at other profiles that are creating content that are creating videos about the same topic. For example, if you are passionate about basketball, take a look at other basketball talents. You can search, for example, basketball and different keywords there, and then you will find videos.

Then take a look at the videos that are getting the most views for them and write down, for example, the ideas that they are using or save them into your mind. And later on, you can use the same video ideas in your videos to get thousands of views. And actually I used this strategy and I got like 1000 first followers in one week or something like that. More than one million views in the last two weeks. When I looked, hey, people are talking about these things, I'm going to create similar videos and then one million views in two weeks just by starting, do you think I took it as a complete beginner. So this is not complicated. Simply do what is already working.

So once you have created your profile, you have chosen your topic and you have a couple of other videos that are talking about the same topic that you want to talk about. The first step is to leave a link to your profile. And with this link you are actually going to earn money. You can leave a link, for example, to a YouTube channel or Instagram, but you can also leave a link to some other website. Let's say, for example, that you are passionate about pianos and you talk about pianos on your TikTok profile. Then you can leave a link to the Amazon website, for example, where they are selling pianos. When somebody clicks the link on your TikTok profile, they go to Amazon.

You can start earning money when people are shopping on Amazon. And that's, Of course, just a simple example of, for example, the guy who was talking about history. He had left a link to his YouTube channel. And now when people come to his YouTube channel, he can start earning money from ads and maybe he has some history Books. So there are many different ways you can earn money, but leave some links, some relevant links to your TikTok profile that will earn you money later on. This process is called affiliate marketing, and I can link to other videos where you can learn more about making money by just leaving links on the Internet. And now the fifth step suit, your first bid.

OK, this might sound scary, but actually this can be very simple because you have already seen other people what kind of videos they are creating or TikTok, what kind of videos are getting lots of use so you can simply pick some of their ideas created in your own way and shoot the quick video. I remember your first video. Don't need to be perfect. Your first 100. We don't need to be. Perfect, simply publish your first video, second video, and you can improve as the time will, soon you will get the data, you will see the numbers, what is working, what is not working. The most important thing is to get started. And usually with stock, as with other social media, if you do what is already working for others, you will most likely get lots of views and followers because you don't need to reinvent the wheel.

You can simply do what has been proven to work, and if it works for others, it will most likely work for yourself as well. Once you have shot your video that takes maybe 15 seconds to 60 seconds, you are ready to publish your video. And this is really exciting. Now, before you publish your video, I recommend that you do this with some background music to your video. It will boost views, people will click more likes and they will share it with their friends and also add some hashtags in your video description. So ad, for example, five to seven hashtags and some good hashtags that I recommend that you use are if Y p then for you and for you pates.

When you use those three hashtags, your Bednall will most likely show up on other people's pages for you to pay so it will get more reviews and then also add some relevant hashtags that tell a little bit what your video is all about. For example, if you talk about history and the Second World War like that one man was doing, put the hashtag Second World War and history. For example, when I talk about making money or lying or finances, are these things about hashtag like money or hashtag, how to make money online? So simply add a couple of hashtags that relate to your video. So that's the basic process of making money through TikTok. You simply need to create your profile and then upload videos.

And once you have done that, then you'll have to repeat, upload videos, upload the videos, upload new videos, and they can be very short like 15 seconds. I know a person who made thousands of dollars with a short 30 second video. One important thing that I recommend you to keep in mind is to create videos about the same topic, about the same subject, because I see some people, they first talk about, for example, music, then they talk about basketball. Then history is jumping from one topic to another topic and all kinds of topics. It makes it confusing for the followers to follow your videos and then they will unfollow and then they will not probably buy the product. They will not earn money in the process. So pick that one topic and stick to it.

For example, I have a friend called Thomas Garrets and hit these people how to make money online and he creates different videos where he shows different ways to earn money from home. So he has created what I'm recording in this video. Twenty four different videos where he simply says side hustle number one. Well, this is how you can make some side income online. The inside has nothing to do with this, how you can earn money online. Then the site has a number three. So he's simply sowing different ways for people to earn money from home and in one do his source one way. Then in the second window, he saw the second way to make money.

So it's about the same topic. Or as I told you about this History Channel, first he talks about the Second World War, then about the First World War, then about Napoleon. So about different things regarding that same topic. And sometimes people ask, OK, well, my topic is, for example, playing guitar. What should I talk about? Like playing guitar? I don't know how to play guitar. Well, one thing that will guarantee that you will never, ever, ever run out of ideas is to pick, for example, ten different profiles, then save them, write them down on the paper or, for example, in your computer or on your mobile phone. Write them down those TikTok profiles and always take ideas from them, see what they are doing.

You will never run out of ideas. Of course, you don't need to copy and paste everything you can, add your own spice, make a little bit of something different, but get ideas. Then you will never need to be creative. You can simply do what is already working. I repeat the process. It's not. It's nothing complicated. I always like to tell people how to make money. It's not complicated. It's simple you to do what is already working and then you start earning money and people who are starting now and they are saying that it's easier to make money on this book than anything that they have ever experienced. For example, if you take out the Lincoln script and you will see, take Thornhill, Jonathan Montoya, Matt Stein and other people, they were struggling to create utopia.

They were blogging, trying all kinds of things to make money online. It was taking a lot of time, a lot of effort, but they were not really getting results. But then they went to TikTok and they started earning like thousands, some of them even more than ten thousand dollars with just little effort on TikTok. And their mind was blown out. And now they are also facing other people on how to do the same. I know personally, maybe ten to twenty people who have tried. And all of them, all of them have said that it works surprisingly well, like it has blown my mind, like it's working better than I could have expected.

And also, when I carried my first DeCock videos, I thought, OK, this is not going to work very well. I probably won't get much views, but I was like, well, I got like one million views in like two weeks after I started seriously creating some videos. So there is a lot of potential on TikTok if you have missed something like Facebook or Instagram or YouTube, or other threats. Now, there is a lot of potential and I have seen it, I can guarantee it from my own experience. That being said, I want to remind you that don't try to create maybe five videos or something like that.

Commit yourself to a look, for example, for one month or three months or one year even, because usually in the long run, you will get the results and everything will build on top of each other. Like if you don't get results with the first five videos, don't worry, create 500 videos. And I guarantee you you will get some results, you will make some money. And there's so much potential with this platform at the moment that I cannot comprehend. Of course, it's not like getting rich quick, but then you cannot print money like that. But I can guarantee there is a lot of potential. I have seen you on many other platforms, but there is a lot of potential.

From 0 to $10,000: YouTube vs TikTok

You can make money worldwide for 100 percent free on YouTube and stock, you can do this anywhere in the world. So which one would be better if we would like to start from complete zero and make ten thousand dollars, which one would be faster and easier for you to make money, YouTube or thick book? With both of these platforms, your earning potential will basically be unlimited. It means that you can earn as much money as you want and you can make money simply by using your smartphone or your laptop. So you don't need a lot of equipment. So let's make a deal. Give me five minutes and I'll teach you exactly how you can make money with TikTok and YouTube, and I will give you the information that will help you decide which one is better for you for making money, YouTube or Taketo.

Give me five minutes. And if you don't even have five minutes, I guess you don't have the patience to make money with these platforms because it takes a little bit of work. All right. Do we have a deal? You watch this for five minutes and if you didn't learn anything, you can close this window. But if you learn something, you will smack the like button and share this video with your friends so they can start making money online as well. All right. So first, let's start with YouTube. This has been around for more than 15 years. People have been making money on YouTube for years. And if you have checked out my other videos, you already know there are many different ways you can make money on YouTube.

The easiest way is probably through YouTube ads. So when you publish a new video on YouTube, YouTube will pay you when they saw some ads before that video or, for example, mentioning someone's product in your videos, the company may pay you money for that. Or you can leave a link, a description of your video. When somebody clicks that and they go somewhere, they buy something. You can earn money for that. So there are many different ways you can make money on YouTube and YouTube has lots of benefits. I will dive into those in a moment. But first, let me briefly explain to you how to make money and TikTok. So making money with TikTok works in a somewhat similar way as with YouTube, but there are some differences.

TikTok is a much faster platform. It also means that you can make money probably even faster on TikTok. What do you need to do is to pick a topic, then leave some link in your profile. People are going to click and go to and when they go there and if they buy something, for example, you can earn money for that. And the videos can be very short like 15 seconds. It can take 30 seconds for you to create and publish a new video and that can make you money. I know a person who made thousands of dollars with just one 30 second video. But now let's dive more into detail. What are the differences between YouTube and Tic-Tac so you can define which one is better for you? Or if you start making money by using both of them like I am doing myself.

First, let me give this to five huge benefits of TikTok and five benefits of YouTube. Let's start with TikTok. Some people call this lazy man's platform to make money online because you can be lazy and make money on, to be honest. And if you take out the link in the description, some people, they spend hours, they put a lot of effort on trying to make money with other platforms. Then they start with TikTok and they start earning money faster by putting in much less effort. So that's why we call this lazy man's platform for making money. So the first benefit is that it's very fast to create videos. If you want to create YouTube videos, sometimes you can create them faster. Sometimes it takes a little bit more time. But we TikTok.

You can literally create a new video in like fifteen seconds to a maximum of sixty seconds. So it's really fast to create videos on this platform. It's not time consuming like many other strategies. Second benefit is that it's easier to get followers and views on TikTok than, for example, on YouTube or Instagram or some other platforms. There are several reasons for that. I'm going to dive into those in a moment. But for example, when I created my first serious video, it took only one week to get 1000 followers. The same talk from like going from zero to 1000 on other platforms. It would have taken like a month. So TikTok is a really fast platform. And also I got more than one million views in two weeks when I published my first serious video.

So you can get views and followers fast if you know what you are doing. Benefit number three is that making money processes is also very simple and simply creates short 15 second videos. You have a link in your description, for example, to some products or Amazon or some website, and then you can earn money by doing that. It's very simple and straightforward. And as they used to say, even a five year old kid or 90 year old grandmother. Could learn the process of making money on TikTok and benefit. Number four is that it's growing extremely fast. TikTok has been the fastest growing social media platform in the whole world during the last months and years. And now it's really hot and trending. Like many people, they say. I hope I would have started on Facebook when it was new.

I hope I would have started using Instagram when it was new, or I would have started on Snapchat or other platforms. But TikTok, it's so fast growing now that the potential is huge. There are so many people on TikTok and they are not only very young people, there are also some elderly people on the platform. And that brings us to our benefit. Number five, there is not much competition. If you go to Instagram, if you go to YouTube, if you go to Facebook, you will see tons of competition. There are thousands and thousands and thousands of influencers trying to compete for attention and especially for beginners and people who are starting out. It can be really hard to gain some traction.

But on TikTok, there is much, much less competition. I have created videos on YouTube. I like more than 500 videos on YouTube to learn how to make honest money online. And I know from experience that there is competition. But when I go to TikTok, I see that there is much, much less competition. It is much easier to get views, much easier to get followers on thick nowadays. That's why they also call this opportunity that comes around only very rarely, because if we move forward, for example, five or ten years, there will be for sure much more competition on TikTok. So if you take out the training into description, you can still be one of the first ones to enter the digital platform and start making money there.

And those were the five benefits of TikTok. Let me know what the comments are, if some of those were interesting ones and legs, if you find some new information. But now we are going to dive into five benefits for making money on YouTube, because even though TikTok is right now a hot opportunity for making money, I still use and I still recommend using YouTube as well. First reason is that it's still the second biggest search engine in the world. Google is the biggest one and YouTube is the second biggest one. And who knows if in the future YouTube will be the biggest search engine in the world? People love watching videos and if you create a video today, it can make money for years to come because you can get ranked on YouTube and it can stay on the top. People can search your video and see it over and over and over again.

Unlike with TikTok, the lifetime of one video is much shorter. No tool with YouTube is that it's more established. It's a reliable way to make money online. You have probably seen many people who have made a living with YouTube. You may have seen some people who have even made a fortune. Some people even made millions of dollars with YouTube. So it's a very reliable way to make money. That's actually one reason why people don't take the right away because they are looking for a good one. Should we go there? Should we not go there? But that's one reason why on TikTok there is not so much competition because they recognize that making money on YouTube, it's very straightforward.

They are already making money there, but they are a little bit afraid of TikTok. This opens up an opportunity for you and me. If you want to make money on TikTok, the number three benefit with YouTube is that it's still bigger than TikTok. Even though TikTok is at the moment the fastest growing social media platform in the world, YouTube is still the biggest one and there are still more than one billion, if not even two billion active users on YouTube every single month. And also those people who are using YouTube are in general a little bit older than on TikTok. So from a money perspective, YouTube is still a better one in that sense. And as I mentioned at the beginning, the earning potential with YouTube is literally unlimited.

As I showed you in some of my other videos, Debro Nathan Lucas, they made more than one million dollars just by using YouTube. So, Of course, even though there is competition on YouTube, you can still make tons of money on this platform. The thing is that it usually takes more time with TikTok. You can get started faster. Some people have made even tens of thousands of dollars with little effort. As you can see in the link description with YouTube, it's usually more time consuming and beneficial. No, then I already mentioned before that you can make money with your videos for years to come. Let's say that you create a video today, you publish it to YouTube, that we will continue with your money this year, next year, the year after that, and even for years and years and years to come with TikTok.

On the other hand, the last time is much shorter. So you published a video today. It. No extra money, for example, one week, two weeks, maybe three weeks maximum, but then it's gone like nobody will likely see it. They may see it if they search for that specific tag. But the lifetime in general is much more dramatic than on YouTube. I have a couple of friends, Jake, Thomas and Jonathan, and they were making money on YouTube, but they explained that it was taking a lot of time and some of them were actually struggling on this YouTube platform. Then they start to think that they heard about this opportunity and they started making money faster. And some people still say that YouTube is better. So I would love to hear from you.

Which one do you prefer? Which one are you going to use to make money, YouTube or TikTok? Let me know in the comments below, because I would love to hear from you personally. I will keep on using both because as I explained, you TikTok and YouTube, both of them have some benefits. Let's say, for example, if I would only create videos on Taketo, I would publish 1000 videos and then Tic-Tac would say, hey, we will shut down your account. Everything would be gone. But now, Of course, I create videos on TikTok, also on YouTube. So let's say TikTok goes down. I still have YouTube. That's my philosophy. And the second reason is, Of course, that they complement each other.

You can get people from TikTok to your YouTube videos and also vice versa if you want. But in my perspective, these two platforms work very well together. So you can make money by using both platforms. But what many people are doing is that they publish a YouTube video and then they promote that video on TikTok. They say, for example, here are a couple of things about this video. If you want to learn more, check out my YouTube video there and then they get thousands of uses for their videos.

2 Secrets To Get Tik Tok Followers And Views Fast!

If you read this video and do what I say, getting your first 1000 followers to take is very easy, getting your first one million views, it's very easy making your first ad dollars on TikTok. No problem. Just give me five minutes of your time and I'll explain to you how you can get your first 1000 followers. TikTok very easily. It's just two simple steps that you need to do that you will learn in this video if you find my tips helpful and valuable. I appreciate it if you mess up the likes of them and share this with your friends who also want to make money on TikTok. Let me show you how I got my first one million views on TikTok and 1000 followers very easily. I'll explain what I did and then I'll share what you can do to get it as well.

So let's go back in time. When I first heard about TikTok, I was like, what is this platform like? Are only what young people like. Everybody who is using it is like ten years old or 15 years old. I was like, is this a real platform? Like, can you make money? Can you do anything? That was very skeptical back then. But then I saw some of my friends. They were getting started. Somebody said, hey, I got awesome results. I thought, well, maybe it's just for a short time. Then another person came there. He said, I got awesome results with TikTok. Then the third person, fourth was and I saw so many people getting started that I started thinking there must be something there. But I thought, OK, I will not start it yet. I will see how the platform evolves.

But then I saw more and more people getting into TikTok and all of them said that, well, I knew that this is awesome. But from what I've seen, this has exceeded my expectations. Everybody was loving TikTok. And they say that they got awesome results from them. I was like, man, if all of those people are getting so good results on data, I need at least to try it, because, as you may know, creating videos on TikTok doesn't take a lot of time. You can create videos in 15 seconds, 30 seconds, 60 seconds. It's not time consuming. Anybody can do it. So I thought I would take a closer look at this platform and try it myself. So what I did was, I just published three videos. I didn't really plan those published.

And when I created those three videos, I didn't really put effort into them. I just published them because I wanted to get into the platform and see how it works in practice. And that also motivated me to research a little bit more. So what I did next is that I started looking at a couple of YouTube tutorials. What do you think this is all about? How does the algorithm work? So some basic things. So I understood what this app is all about because as you know, I am not ten years old anymore. So I don't understand it so well as some very young people download the app. They start using it immediately. They understand everything immediately. I was not like them.

I went towards a couple of YouTube tutorials until I understood it. Then I also spent a little bit of time on the app. I was scrolling the videos and I was seeing how it works. And then I saw my friends that I mentioned at the beginning. They were making money on TikTok. They were getting followers, they were getting leads. Everything wonderful was happening to them. Thanks to TikTok, by the way, I believe you linked with groups and for the training where they explain everything, how they did it. So I started taking some notes. I was, OK, they are doing this, then they are doing this. I started taking a look at a couple of their videos that were getting lots of use. Some of the videos were getting more than one million views. Another one was getting hundreds of thousands of uses. So I took notes.

And by the way, this works within any topic. You can create a TikTok profile about any topic simply to see what is already working in the platform and do the same and you will get the results. So I brought them some notes and then I had a list of different kinds of videos that I could create myself that will most likely get good results because I thought if those people are getting good results, I can get good results as well. And that time I didn't have any serious videos on my tech platform, only those three videos that I published like that. And then came the time that I published my first, let's say, serious video. It takes maybe one minute or two minutes to create, not much, because I had already seen that other people are creating this kind of video.

So I decided I want to create a similar video as well, and that we got like seventy thousand views like that. And it got hundreds of comments, hundreds of likes and lots of engagement. Then I created a couple of other videos and my first serious video. It got more than 600,000 views, thousands of comments, and thousands of likes. And then I was like, man, this is really working. I just took a look at what other people are doing and I do the same now. I'm getting tons of views. I'm getting tons of comments, tons of engagement. Wow. This is wonderful. And that's actually what a lot of people have done with TikTok. And that's what I recommend to you. Do what is already working on the platform. I leave a link. It is a group where we can learn more details about what is already working in the.

From there, my friends will explain to you what works for them, how to create a perfect profile, how to find perfect videos, and how to never run out of ideas. They will explain all of this to you. But in a nutshell, the process like this is two steps. You simply take a look at other people's videos within your topic. So, for example, if you are talking about basketball, you take a look at five to 10 basketball profiles, see what kind of videos are getting good results for them, and then you create similar kinds of videos. Of course, those two steps are just the basics of this thing. Like, Of course, there are more details into that and you will learn more in that training that you find in the description. But that's basically the process.

You don't need to reinvent the wheel. You see what is working for others and then you do the same. I did this and I got one million views in just two weeks and 1000 first followers in just one week. And as I told you, I didn't have any prior experience. I was not technically savvy. I didn't like anything special. I just saw what was working and I did the same. And now you might be asking, hey, Robert, can it really be so easy? And my answer is yes. Getting followers and views is easy, but there are three mistakes that I see some people making, so you must avoid them. I'm going to reveal this to you right now. But if you are enjoying it so far, remember the success of the likes, let me know in the comments which one of these tips is most valuable. So the first mistake that I see people making is that they quit immediately.

They give up immediately or they don't even get started. Most people never get started. That's why they don't make money on TikTok and out of those people who get started. Most people just published maybe one or three videos and then they quit. So when you are getting started and when you follow this strategy, you see what is working and you do the same, then you just need to do it for a while. For me, it started working immediately, but for some people it may take some while. So don't quit. Instead of committing to publish just let's say, five or 10 videos, commit to publishing at least 50 videos. I'm 100 percent sure that you will get some results. The second mistake is not adding background music. Of course, this is what is simple.

You can simply fix this. So just as background music and if you add background music, make sure that it's not too noisy, you can adjust the background music and your own words. What I personally like to use within the app, I put the background music level at something like seven to 10, quite low and then my own voice volume 100 or something like that. So do a background volume. It's only in the background that it says. So it's not something too noisy. Then the third mistake that some people make is not adding haystacks. Of course, I'm not saying that you cannot get views without adding haystacks, but adding haystacks will definitely help you to get more views. What I recommend you do is add three to seven haystacks for every single video that you publish on TikTok unless you have some good reason.

Alright, so those were two three quick chapters. How you can improve your videos and get that first 1000 followers faster. But then the mistake I have seen a lot of people making is that they don't think about how to make money or TikTok. I've seen people who had hundreds of thousands of followers or even tens of thousands. I've seen this on other platforms, on YouTube, on Instagram. There are people who have so many followers, and have so many subscribers. They have all the potential in the world, but they haven't thought about how to make money. They have all they are leaving money on the table. So don't do this with Dicterow. Don't just have tens of thousands of followers and not have any strategy with that.

How are you going to monetize it, because that is going to help your followers, for example, leave a link to some relevant product, into your profile. When people go and buy that product, you will earn money for that. And your followers, they will benefit. They will learn something from the product. So you will be happy for earning money and your followers will be happy because they will get some extra. They will get some product that can improve their results, that can give them some benefit. So as you are building your profile, I always want you to keep in mind, like the end results, how you are going to monetize this. And Of course, that's also one option that you don't want to touch its users really for fun. But I would say that in many cases you can make money relatively easily if you have a following already. Of course not. In all cases it's a ton of money, but at least something. And by providing helpful products, you can also help your followers and your audience.

5 Ultra-Powerful Tips to Make Even MORE Money on TikTok!

If you want to make money on TikTok, you are in the right video because today I will give you five EU secrets that will help you to make more money on TikTok. And these secrets are so easy to use that even a seven year old kid can use these to make even more money on TikTok. And if you're going to do even tip number one, you are going to fail. So you need to listen very closely to follow the advice, number one. And then advice number five is extremely important because if you don't do that, you are destined to fail. So what is very close to the end? And let's go right the way to the tip number one, which is not having an offer. This is so big. Mistakes are so many people have, like I've seen it, to stock profiles with 50000 followers or 100000 followers. So let's say 20000 followers, but they don't have anything to offer like they are leaving so much money on the table.

Of course, money may not be the only thing that is important. Of course not. It's not the only two that are important. But that may also help their viewers, because you may promote on your TikTok profile some products that may be helpful for them. So you are not only making money, but you can also help your followers to achieve something that they want to achieve. Let's say, for example, that you have a fitness profile and are ticked off. You publish with us about fitness topics and then you have 20000 followers, but you don't have anything to promote. You are leaving money on the table.

Let's say a simple example are you are using, for example, some protein powder that helps you to be in good shape and build some muscle, for example, simply leaving a simple link in your TikTok profile saying people click here if you want to buy the best protein powder, that is already going to make you some money if you have a lot of followers. So simple, simple things like five seconds to do it. Or Of course, you can have different kinds of offers. You can take people to your Instagram profile and you may have some offers there. But I've seen some people having 100,000 followers and then they have a link to their Instagram profile, but they don't promote anything. They're like they don't have any offers because if you want to make some money, you need to have some offer.

Of course, if you want to do things like you don't want to make any money, that's all completely fine. You don't need to do it like this, only if you want to make some money, then you need to have some of it. If you don't have any of your own products, you can promote other people's products or simply copy and paste the link. When people click it and buy something, you earn a lot more money to tip number one, which is to be consistent, like when you start or anything like it, whether to stick to it when you start reading a book. If you want to make money on top of blogging or whatever you want to do, you need to start with the long term perspective. Like what do you really want to achieve? Is it like some people say, OK, I'll just try this. I published five videos.

If it doesn't work, I quit. Most likely they are going to quit because with your first wife videos, most likely you are not going to make success like you need to have this long term finance perspective and you need to be consistent over the long term. So if you are starting to take stock, I would say that you have a goal to publish at least 100 videos. And then when you are publishing those videos, you can always analyze what is working and you can analyze this on TikTok Analytics. If you have this account, by the way, it's one person free to have the TikTok pro account. And then you simply analyze what kind of videos are getting the most views, what kind of videos are getting the most comments, and what kind of videos are getting the most likes. And then you can create similar videos to your audience.

You can get even more views and even more likes and even more engagement. And eventually you can also help the more influence. People are more anonymous to also make more money. So once you consistently keep on uploading new videos to publish new videos, sooner or later you start seeing, OK, this video got tons of views. One powerful thing that you can do on TV is to read and upload the same video later. Of course, don't reupload it immediately. But let's say wait for example, one month, then you re-upload the same video. And now if you are asking like, can this really work? Yes, I've seen many big YouTube videos. Even people like Gary Vaynerchuk, who is like a multimillionaire, like this media mogul, like Cute's entrepreneur, he is even using it and many other successful entrepreneurs are using it. So it works.

So let me give you an example from my own Tic-Tac profile. I had no, we do not get one point six million views. I was like, hey, this was very successful. So I could say we do. I simply copy paste, upload the same video with the same description, same everything. And that got more than one million views, even though usually my other videos get like maybe 10000 views, some 50000 views, some 5000 views. This got one million views, even though it was re-uploading because again. Most of your subscribers and followers haven't seen your old videos, and also there are other people who haven't seen your video, so when you reapply it, more people will see it. And your followers who didn't see it for the first time, they will see it now.

But again, don't overuse it later. Don't upload every single video, only summer. OK, some people have said they have uploaded the same. We do like even three times or the time Book if they have been on take or even four times. Again, you need to use some common sense with this, but this is a powerful strategy that works. It's like low effort, but it can provide higher results. So it's really powerful. Tip number four is that it is so easy that anybody can reply to comments, because when you reply and like people's comments, they will see that, hey, this is a real person, this is communicating here and that builds trust. They start trusting you more. They want to follow you more. They want to watch more of your videos.

Maybe they want to buy your offers even more. And then they start to say, hey, this guy is replying this is a great person, or it also encourages people who see your video. They say, hey, this guy is responsible. Maybe we can also ask something from him. Maybe you can also comment because he's reading the comments. And again, if you don't want to do this yourself, if you don't want to, like, spend hours and hours and hours, like replying to comments, you can also hire somebody else to do this for you. You can pay somebody, let's say, some money, and they will answer some comments for you. For example, myself, I like answering comments when I'm in the gym as a scroll. My article, I see what people are answering me and I reply to comments.

It's just something fun. Like it doesn't take a lot of time to do. It's just reading a couple of comments replying, but it's really seeing your orders that you read and you care and it really builds trust. So this is what it is to do. A deal with Bennett was number five is extremely important. I've seen many especially like it, let's say younger people falling into this mistake that they don't think about so much what their viewers want to see. They simply publish what is interesting and important for them. But that is the wrong attitude to get started, to dictate, you need to get started from the perspective, like what can you provide for people and what are other people interested in seeing? Because eventually you are not creating those videos for yourself.

Afterwards you are creating them for other people towards interesting sterilizes. I saw one desktop user was using that. He asked sometimes in Sweden, what do you want to see next? And then people commented there, like they say, hey, can you create this kind of weather, can create this kind of window. And then people like that comment and it goes, hi, this is OK. My followers want to see me creating this kind of window. Then he delivers and then again he asks, what do you want to say next? And then people say to him, We want to say this and this. And then he creates that kind of freedom. And then he can basically keep on doing this forever and ever. He never needs to create like her own ideas. He never needs to, like, be creative. He simply asks from his followers what kind of videos you want and then he creates that. And that is like people love it because then he's doing something for other people. So that is something important. Focus on your viewers and your followers rather than what you want to see.

4 Ways to Find Lucrative Affiliate Programs That Pay Up to $1,000 Per

A lot of you have been asking me how to find affiliate programs that make tons of money easily. So in this video, I'm going to show you how you can find lucrative affiliate programs that pay you even 1000 dollars like this and this and this. So what's under the end? Because we are starting right away. We are wondering what is an affiliate program or this affiliate marketing? It's simply a process of making money by promoting someone else's product so you can promote products on Amazon or any other website. Now, you may ask how to find those products to promote like you don't need to create any own products. You can just promote somebody else's products and you can earn even 1000 dollars like this. So how to find those products and how to find good products for promotion? Well, I'm going to give you four strategies in this video. I'm using it myself.

And the first wave that I recommend you to do is think about the products that you are using yourself. So, for example, I was using this product called Thrive PIMS and Pizza. These were two examples from my own life. And I was thinking, hey, these are wonderful products. Why would I recommend these to other people as well? So a lot of people will, for example, ask me what is a good WordPress plugin or WordPress theme? And I was already using this product that was almost like a credit. The video when I saw the best WordPress theme for affiliate marketing and I mentioned strike themes there. And this is how I naturally was able to promote a product that I was already using myself and that other people were wanting to use because they were asking what is the best team for affiliate marketing? So I was using product people or needing it.

I said, hey, this is what I use. This is great. You could use it also or let's say that you are playing football or let's say you are swimming or whatever your needs are, your topic. Think about the things that you are using to develop products that you are using. Could you promote and recommend them to your friends also? Or let's say that you are with the photograph, you need two cameras, you are using some specific camera and you love it. It's wonderful. Or some microphone. Could you promote it to other people? So in that need as well, because most of the products that I promote, I am using them myself. Let me give you another example. This is a platform where you can create and sell online Books. And I created an online Book on this platform.

I made some money doing that. And then I noticed that they also have this affiliate program and they say, can we send a check for you every month? And I was like, wow, hey, why wouldn't I just promote this product to other people as well? I may even get a hundred dollars commision for one sale because it pays you every single month. So this is something great that if you are using some products, you can promote them to other people as well, because then it's also easier for you to promote the sale because you have already sold it to yourself. So that's the first word. By the way, I believe you. Linklaters groups and where I have explained three different threads is how to find affiliate programs. These are easy ways.

This is what I believe. You think about LinkedIn and where you can read it through. Now let's move to the next one. So right on Google, for example, you need affiliate programs. So let me give you some examples. Let's say that you are a travel blogger or you are in the travel industry and you inspire other people to travel and you want to earn money by doing that. Here you can go to Google based affiliate programs for travel bloggers and it will give you dozens and dozens and dozens of different ideas. Let me show you a list of travel affiliate programs for travel bloggers, exactly what you are looking for, nine of our highest earning travel affiliate programs. Then you can click it and open and see what's inside 25 top affiliate programs.

To Toyin, as a travel blogger, or let's say that you are a luxury traveler, AMSOIL looks for a travel affiliate, programs you can type on Google simply type your needs. So luxury travel and then affiliate programs. And this applies to the Internet, whether it's football, basketball or, let's say, jogging or lifting weights or whatever. You can find affiliate programs simply by using this strategy. Then you scroll down and you can see twelve affiliate programs for traveling ten, seven, ten, so many different affiliate programs that you can use. And then you take a look at them. You can open some twelve luxury travel affiliate programs, even 1000 pounds. But keep in mind, this is one eleven one thousand pounds, not a dollar. So you may only have one month, five hundred dollars for one thing like this. So this is something exciting.

You can read through, you can upload affiliate programs. And let me show you an example. They already have links, but if you want to find affiliate programs, you can simply copy and paste the name of the company and type on Google affiliate programs. So I mentioned it to you at the. Beginning of this trial with themes, so when I wanted to search for their affiliate programs to start promoting them, I brought here a private theme, an affiliate program, and then it was so you hear it was an attractive affiliate program today. And if you open this page, well, it explains in detail how you can make money. So they pay 35 commission per purchase and then also recover Comisión. Komisar means that you will earn money every single time when somebody renews the purchase.

So, for example, I'm also promoting this affiliate and they have monthly memberships. So every time somebody renews their monthly membership, I earn commissions. And some people, they say, stay there for years and years and years. So I keep earning commissions every single month and every single year. And the same is with the trial teams as well. And the person that is simple, Of course, if you earn 35 percent per commission, it will be four out of 100 dollars. That will obviously be 35 dollars. Now, if you're asking, hey, where to find those that pay one thousand dollars per sale, let me soil let me go forward in this strategy. When you come here to a wealthy affiliate, this one out of these three strands is in my article here.

You've come to a wealthy affiliate, I believe, description, and then you click here on the left side affiliate programs. And here you can find tons of different affiliate programs. And they show you here how big commissions you will be earning. For example, volumes are paying you 2000 dollar commission trading at its one thousand eight hundred seventy dollars commission Yahoo! Small, up to one thousand five dollars commission. Botibol, up to 800 doodlers. So here you can see and then you can use this filtering here. You can filter out different things that a commission price here, for example, the rating, because other members here, there are nine million members at one point. They are reviewing these things. So here you can choose your needs.

Your category, for example, has unwitnessed clothing and the categories, department store associates, women and so on and so forth. Let's say that you would like to earn 2000 dollar commissions for this. You can say that it has received good reviews, 4.5 stars out of five. There are 23 comments. You can talk with other members here today, with other people. Casoni says it's excellent. So you have people who have been writing the reviews and you have to explain how everything works. And you can join this program simply by clicking this story in this program. And then it will take you to this place where you can fill out your application and get started with this affiliate program. This, for example, is in the CSA affiliate network.

So you need to become a member therefore completely free worldwide again. OK, let's move to the next way to make money online and how to find affiliate programs. Let me. So you follow influencers and competitors within your needs and see what they are promoting. So let me give you an example. If you are in a tennis need, you are promoting tennis products you can find on Google and on YouTube, tennis, tennis or tennis websites. So, for example, this tennis warehouse, take a look at their videos. What are they promoting, what kind of products they promote to other people? And then you will get ideas or let's say this website, Tennis Channel, you can see the products they are promoting on top speed tennis. You can see the rackets, all different kinds of products they are promoting.

Get ideas from other people in units or let me , for example, legendary marketer, how I found this affiliate program. As I saw here in the video, I made 3000 dollars in a day. They paid big commissions, as you can see. Two thousand dollars for one sale, one thousand dollars for one sale. I found this program because many people in my industry make their money online. But they were promoting this. They were saying, let the market. That is great. It teaches you how to build an online business even without any experience. And you can scale your online business if you already have one. So I was like, hey, I want to take a closer look at it. So I joined this program. I've paid a lot of product prices and whatever.

And then I went through the training. I spent like two months researching the program, if it's really worth promoting. And then I went, hey, this is a great program. I want to promote it also. So then I went out, I started promoting and as you can see, I made even three thousand dollars in one day with my record with this program, but where you can also get started with it, I believe in the description you're online that comes 3000. So these were four ways you can find lucrative affiliate programs: following other people in units, thinking about the products that you are using yourself, simply type in a Google for other affiliate programs and then using this wealthy affiliate affiliate program.

Platform by clicking here. So these are the Fawwaz, let me know in the comments with one of these Fawwaz you are going to use to start finding lucrative and high paying affiliate programs.

Let me also know in the comments from which country you are from. So I will give you more different ways to make money in your country. These ways that I showed you with this would be available worldwide in the United States, Philippines, India, anywhere. Thank you very much for reading. And we will see you in the next video.

My Story - How My Account Got BANNED Because of Bullies on TikTok

You are probably reading this window because your thick account has been banned and you are thinking how to get on TikTok. I got banned from a thick book with more than 50000 followers, but later I got my account recovered following the steps that I will reveal to you in this video. Tell me in the comments. If you have also been banned on TikTok, I have some good news and bad news for you. Let's start with the good news: you may get your account recovered if you do what I tell you in this video. The bad news is that you may not hear back from TikTok for several days, so you must follow the instructions that I explain in this video.

Where do you read it closely? Before I read through the steps on how to get on the bump on TikTok, let me tell you a little bit of background and how I got banned. And then abundantly clear, perhaps you can relate with my story a little bit. Some time ago, TikTok suddenly banned my account. I just woke up in the morning, I grabbed my phone and I went to Tik Tok. And it said that my account has been permanently banned at more than 52000 followers, and I was getting 200 to 450000 views per day. And now all of that is gone. Why was I banned from TikTok? I can summarize it in three words. I got bullied. Let me tell you in a nutshell, what happened? So I created an ultra popular trend in the Phoenix speaking TikTok, because Feeney's is my native language.

So I was creating big windows in Phoenix, and then many people started creating videos with the same theme. There was a specific music and then a specific idea with all of those videos. First, the person is like a depressed old man. Tomorrow I need to go to work. Then you realize you make money by smiling and everything is great. So it was kind of encouraging people to start making money online. And if they calculate all the views that these kinds of videos got on TikTok, they got millions and even tens of millions of views because many people were creating videos within this thread and tens of millions of views.

For all of those videos and opinions, language is quite the lot. Because of penises, the small language step number one was that Finnish people started to become jealous because they thought I could add this ultraportable out of print. I was making money online and I had to become successful. And I don't know how much you know about Finnish culture, but it's different from, for example, in the United States, where success is something good. If somebody becomes a successful entrepreneur, it's something great in Phoenix culture, better life. If somebody succeeds a lot, they become jealous, they become angry.

That's why is this one person succeeding that I am not? So many Finnish people thought of creating all kinds of fake stories about me because they were jealous. They made up all kinds of crazy stories. For example, somebody told me I took the robust thing online and immediately €800 disappeared from my bank account. This kind of crazy story doesn't even make any sense unless you know many people and think they are young kids. So they started believing those fake stories and they started spreading those fake rumors about me. And obviously, nobody had any proof for those fake stories of fake claims because they will lie.

But at this point, people didn't need any proof. They just thought that hating, hating on me. Of course, there were a lot of my supporters. My followers will know that what I teach is true. They have followed my steps and made money online and all these kinds of things. But there were so many new people who have never heard of me, and the first thing they heard about me were those fake rumors, so they became extremely mad without any reason. So I started getting more and more amused every day.

Some people were really supporting me. They said, You are talking, you are legit. The people are also supportive towards me and some people who are blaming those fake rules. They were like, No, we must take this into account. And they started mass reporting. I started getting like 450000 views in a single day on TikTok, and that is a lot. It means that almost every single person in Finland who is using take saw my video in those days and people started shouting all kinds of nasty words and they started bullying me on TikTok a lot. It was crazy, and some people started reporting a cold without any good reason. And as a result, TikTok took my account down. It got banned from stock. So how did I get my account recovered? Let me explain to you what happened.

How to RECOVER Your TikTok Account Step-By-Step

So I went through YouTube, I started researching how to get on the bed and think, look how to recover my account. And I saw lots of YouTube videos from many people's experiences, and many of them actually told that they got their first account banned. And then after a couple of days, they got it on the band and they explained to the tapes what they did in order to do that. Someone thought that she got her TikTok back in three days. Another person got her account back in four days. Somebody got her account back in six days. It was right. It was around three to six days and these people got their accounts recovered. One interesting thing was that big never told those people why their accounts had been banned in the first place.

And TikTok did tell me either at this point. So I started sending claims to TikTok, and I will explain where you'll need to send those claims in order to recover at this point when my account is down. Many people often think of my follow ups, they give to my YouTube channel here and they tell me, Hey, come back, take we miss you, we want you back. So I thought, Hey, I will create a new account. Meanwhile, I'm trying to get my old account back, and that's also a tip for you. Create a new account. Meanwhile, because many people who followed your old account, they will most likely follow your new account as well. And it's just five short days.

I got more than 600 than afforded thousand views in total for the new account and more than four thousand followers. So many people found my new account that there was a lot of hype around that. At this point, I realized that I had probably spent too much time on TikTok, and that'll probably focus on other parts of the old building of an online business. And that's also advice for you. If you are doing an online business, make money online to learn also many other ways to make money online because one way is to make money on a big book and that is great. You can impact many people positively, but you should not rely on TikTok because even though you may get your account recovered following the steps that I'm about to reveal to you, you still should diversify a little bit your online income streams.

So I would leave you all the resources in the description where you can find no old. But now let's move the steps, how I got my account recovered. So it took more than one week to get my account recovered. I remember it was Tuesday morning when I took it, my account was gone. And then still, after one week next Tuesday, my account will still sit down. And in fact, I heard from TikTok. And this was one of the reasons why I was almost certain I would not get my account back because I had gone to a TikTok feedback page. I will actually leave your link in the description where you're going to go to the page and then you're going to fill out the claim and you can explain what has happened and why you should get your account recovered.

Recode explains them in detail, but also in a short way, so it doesn't take so much time for them to read it. And you may send this message. It's several times. I sent it a couple of times, and I saw many other people had sent the message because of many problems and they got the account recovered, another way where we can go is to go to TikTok and then create a new account and record their report of a problem and then click a profile page. And then you can also fill out the feedback form and then Bigfoot will get your feedback and they can reply to you. So after five days, I heard back home think, Look, I got an email. I don't know if this was from a real human being or from the book, but it said, Thanks for contacting me.

Think we all understand how important your card is to you? After periods of review, your account will remain permanently banned due to a violation of our violent extremism policy. I was like, what? My account has never, ever, ever what I had seen violated. That's kind of like violent extremism policy. Therefore, I send even more request to think I reply to that message will be received from them. I went back to the website to fill out the feedback from and also the big book app went to report the problem to the profile page. And then I did that again and again a couple of times and then after eight days. So my TikTok account was banned on Tuesday and the next week.

On Wednesday, after eight days, someone sent me a message on WhatsApp and said, Hey, it seems that you'll recover the account. So I looked into TikTok and I saw the following methods for their team. Your appeal was reviewed. Thank you for submitting your request. We apologize for any inconvenience this may have caused. Thank you for being a part of the community in a nutshell. People say that. Sorry that we're about to hear your account back.

2 TIPS for TikTok

Here are two important points that you want to really remember if your account has ever been banned or if it has even been banned. First of all, don't put too much effort on your TikTok account because they made barnyard cold without any reason, any time they wanted to make money on other platforms as well. For example, on YouTube, blogging started building an email list. I think about all these kinds of things on this channel. I will help you to make money online. And second, keep on sending messages to the tech support on their feedback form and also through their app. Because this is what I did and this is what many other people did, who got their accounts recovered. Now, at the time when I'm recording this video, something strange is still going on on TikTok.

First of all, TikTok raised the death of my username overnight. I don't know what happened. Then it also said that I cannot test my bias on my profile for a full two or three days. So all kinds of strange things are happening on TikTok, and that's a stronger reason why you should also focus on other platforms to make money online. That being said, I'm still going to use TikTok to build an online business, make money online and also inspire other people to do the same. If you want to learn step by step how to make money on them, I believe a link to the description that helped me a lot to make the above Dole lost on TikTok over time.

www.ingramcontent.com/pod-product-compliance
Lightning Source LLC
Chambersburg PA
CBHW072054230526
45479CB00010B/1059